Healing Your Money Mindset

"Kingdom Principles to heal mentally, emotionally, spiritually, and financially to live a prosperous life."

ISBN 978-1-953788-72-6 (Printed)

Healing Your Money Mindset

"Kingdom Principles to heal mentally, emotionally, spiritually, and financially to live a prosperous life."

Jeanette V. Barnette

Table of Contents

Dedication

To my mom, Sharon Barnette-Davis, and my bonus dad Craig Davis, for taking care of me, raising me to be a rising star, and never allowing me to settle for anything less.

To my little sister Sharyn Barnette, my biggest cheerleader, who always believes in me and supports every idea I have, no matter how crazy it is.

To my pastors/shepherds, Bishop Christopher and Dr. Melissa Clark, for being my teachers, preachers, and leaders. For constantly pushing me to become who God created me to be.

To my coach Alexandria Harris for always telling me the truth even when it hurt, never giving up on me, and lighting a passion and a fire in my soul that I never knew I had.

To all my friends and family who constantly surround me with love and support daily.

To everyone who reads this book, may it change your mind and life.

Introduction

This book is for faith-based individuals struggling with their money mindset due to factors like cultural history, lack of knowledge, financial traumas, life's trials, tribulations, situations, and circumstances. This book will cover understanding your money mindset, a poverty mindset, an abundance mindset, understanding your relationship with money, assessing your feelings about money, basic budgeting, essential credit, saving money plans, paying off debt, and speaking life over your finances. Life situations, my own experiences, my client's experiences, and tons of conversations with my family and friends about money have led to me writing this book. This book is for anyone walking in their faith journey who wants to improve their overall mindset, habits, and behavior when it comes to money. I have watched so many people in my culture and community struggle in the area of their finances over the years, and the principles in this book are based on a combination of knowledge, research, analyzing behaviors, and experience to help you in your lifelong journey.

My name is Jeanette Barnette, and I'm certified in financial coaching, life coaching, meditation, and biblical intelligence. I spent 12 years working in the banking and finance industry. Today I coach people through all types of financial situations. I am the founder of a nonprofit organization called The Cultivated Seed. The Cultivated Seed is a growth and development organization that helps our culture and community in the areas of personal and business growth to help them have a better quality of life. I am also the CEO of Kreative Kniche, which provides money, faith, lifestyle products, and digital resources. Although I have received a certain level of prosperity in my life, I have come a long way and have yet to see all the promises God has for me.

I grew up in the hood of the west side of Baltimore, Maryland. The only thing I knew about money as a child was that there was never enough. I don't remember my family ever really talking about money in the household. Growing up, I remember whenever the food stamps would arrive, there was a joy because my family could eat, and it was the only time my sister and I could pick out anything we wanted to eat from the store. In the neighborhood I grew up in, people barely had money to eat and dress decent. Being able to travel the world and build businesses was only a dream. I remember being in church as a young girl and hearing a pastor preach about the promises of God but passing abandoned houses in a neighborhood on our walk back home after church and wondering how God's promises worked because I didn't see it in my community. I was determined to live a better life and see all of God's promises. As a little girl, I read every book I could and let my imagination go wild. I knew at a young age that it was more to life than where I was at that very moment.

I went on to work in the banking and finance industry for 12 years. I held several positions at large banks like Blue Cross and Blue Shield's Credit Union, Bank of America, and Regions bank. I learned about different types of accounts, mortgages, credit, etc. But the most valuable lesson I learned in the banking industry was how people utilized money, resources, and utilized their credit. I consistently analyzed people, their accounts, and their behavior. Day after day, I saw how wealthy-minded people managed their money and how people with a poverty mindset managed their money. The experience I had working in the banking industry was a huge eye-opener, and it helped me navigate through several aspects of life and it helps me as a coach. I couldn't help but notice that the culture and community that struggles the most are African Americans. Even those that made money had a tough time keeping it, but we worked the hardest. There seems to be a mindset rooted in lack that no one talks about in our culture and community that impacts our thoughts, behaviors, and habits, which we have passed down for generations. Well, this belief system ends here and now. The goal of this book is to break generational curses around money by providing simple kingdom principles.

Please be blessed.

Chapter 1

Principles of Understanding Your Money Mindset

"Do not be shaped by this world; instead, be changed within by a new way of thinking."

(Romans 12:2, NCV)

History

Let's talk about our history with money because it's the reality that nobody wants to face the root cause, and many people don't like to talk about the dark past. However, healing comes through revealed truth. If you go back to our history, as African Americans, we are descendants of slaves, which means our ancestors were bought, borrowed, and enslaved for money, work, and resources. The banking system was rooted in slavery, so we never had an ideal mindset of being and generating real wealth. We were always on the property side of that bargaining system. So, no wonder we have issues, misunderstandings, and bad relationships regarding money. It is because we were a part of the very blood of it. I think you must understand that concept and accept that in your heart and mind before moving forward into healing. From society's perspective, the concept of banking and money was never created for our culture to succeed. Knowing that wealth is still our birthright is God's truth. We must get into our heads that we have a right to have money. God has already promised us riches.

Throughout history, some people were still successful when it came to money, building businesses, and building wealth. Madam C.J. Walker created her line of hair care products for African Americans. Once we can get past this belief system that we can't hold onto money or don't have enough money, we can begin building our dream business. I believe that if our ancestors continued to move forward, we can get past anything. Part of healing from something is just starting to have difficult conversations, facing the reality of our history, gathering some understanding, and then moving forward, understanding that our path is still bright despite what happened in the past. And for many African American people, we haven't let go of simply surviving. We work hard, grind, and grit. Still, many African American people either have nothing to show for all the hard work or live in the present moment and spend everything they have, never accumulating money and not truly leaving generational wealth. So, I hope people see money differently after reading this book. I hope everyone owns their responsibility in their situation. Hopefully, people also start teaching the next generations better financial habits and a better money mindset to end the curse. We've been doing this for centuries now. It ends here; we can have wealth and generate wealth conversations in our communities and households and normalize talking about money and success.

Learned Behavior

Let's go back to your childhood and start from there. What was your first memory of money? Think back to the first time you remember receiving money or someone talking about money. What did you learn in that moment? Did you grow up in a wealthy family, or did your family barely make ends meet? Did your parents sit you down and have conversations with you about money? Did you learn about finances in school? Did you learn about money from your friends? Go back and think about this because this was your starting place. It's what drives and motivates your life experiences around money? Were you able to work at an early age or not? How did it feel when you cashed your first check? Our values and beliefs start to form when we are young children. We don't have to sit still long enough to understand why I place money in my bra or under my bed. But odds are we saw someone else do it and associated it with a safe place. So before moving forward, take a moment to think through how you felt about money as a child because understanding is needed before healing can occur. Often, we don't want to relive an experience that may have been traumatic, but these experiences shape the way we think and feel about money. We must identify where the habits formed if we want to see some change.

Autopilot

Our brains are programmed to do what's familiar. We do what has been drilled into us as expected, what we see every day, what we witness every day. Where part of each moment, our brains automatically go to what's expected or comfortable, even if it's not what's best for us. Our brains' main job is not to keep us to be happy. Our brain's main job is to keep us to be safe. Sometimes safe means doing the same thing you already know because you know the outcome. It doesn't mean that what's going to happen will be better than the other side, as crazy as it seems. It means you're familiar with the outcome and know what will happen, so you feel safe. Trying something new, not being aware of the result, is scary. It's no different when it comes to your thoughts and habits around money. A lot of times, we learn what we see, and we mimic what our parents do or did because that's what's familiar. We know what will happen even if we don't fully understand it. We know how certain things will turn out. So, we continue down that road because we know the path already. I remember as a little girl, I would always ask my mom the question why; I still ask why a lot. I am always seeking to understand so I can possibly improve what's not working well.

In my banking career, and even in my career as a financial coach, I have noticed that certain cultures of people do things a certain way and have different results. For example, I remember working at Bank of America, and I would see customers' accounts and information, of course, and some people would have $100,000 available account credit capability. They could borrow $100,000 from the bank and also borrow that money at a 0% interest rate for up to about a year. I have seen other races borrow large sums of money, buy a home, or start a business and double or triple the money they borrowed. They would end up paying that $100,000 loan off before interest starts accruing and then keep the profits.

Now, the reality is I didn't see people in my culture and community having a high enough credit score and available credit line to be able to borrow $100,00, let alone at a 0% interest rate.

When I analyzed and compared the customer accounts, most African American customers could not borrow large sums of money because their credit wasn't in good standing. Most African American customers might have had a $2,500 credit limit, and many were over the credit line, or they may have been close to that limit. They had a 23.99% interest rate, meaning it would take them years to pay off that simple $2,500. As a culture, we tend to live in a debt mindset. We live in a perspective of just borrowing money for the moment for things we don't really need, and we never seem quite able to get ahead and get a profit. Well, a lot of that has to do with our understanding of money, generating wealth, our knowledge of our credit, and our understanding that we deserve to be wealthy and live in the moment. As a culture, we are huge consumers of goods, products, and services. As a culture, we are the number one consumer. Yet we don't have a lot of ownership or investment in the very products that we consume. For example, African American women are the number one consumer of weaves and wigs. However, the hair store supply industry is dominated by the Asian community and is difficult to get into. But why? Building wealth has always been and is still a struggle. Even when we get a form of wealth, we blow it or still don't have anything to leave to the next generation. It doesn't matter the career doesn't matter the choice. It matters the decisions that you make once you have money.

Everything that happens in life happens because of the way we think. Having a money mindset is no different. Thoughts control our belief systems, values, ideas, habits, and behaviors. Before we can heal anything, we must accept that change is needed and deal with the truth instead of covering it up all the time. Our mindset is formed by how we see and experience things in life. Money or lack of can control our emotions and even impact our health. So why don't we talk about it more in our communities? Fear, slavery, bondage, generational curses, I can go on and on, but hopefully, your mindset will change after reading this book. Reality Check: "Thoughts and ideas are living things. Thoughts produce tangible results. I have a powerful long-term effect on your life. Thinking is your greatest gift and is the most vital aspect of your being" Kimbro, Dennis, et al. "'1." Think and Grow Rich: A Black Choice, Fawcett Columbine, New York, New York, 1997, pp. 24.

Society Expectations

We tend to look at the world through a perfect lens and want everything the Jones has because then we think our lives will be perfect. Unfortunately, we live in a society that lives far beyond their means and wants the best name-brand items when we can't even afford them. The reality is I have met several millionaires and managed their bank accounts, and they don't care about flashy items, not name brand. They understand a fundamental concept in the area that our culture struggles with. It is not about how hard you work and how much money you make today.

Ultimately, it is about how much you can keep and how you can make life easier for the next generation. "Good people leave their wealth to their grandchildren, but sinners' wealth is stored up for good people" (Proverbs 13:22, NCV). Are you more worried about what other people think you have or setting your family up for the best financial future possible? The choice is yours. It is my job to expose the truth in this book, and our people have struggled far too long because of the lack of truth and knowledge.

Growing up, we are taught to work and invest in other people's dreams, not our own. There's a lack of shared information in our culture and community. We must break generational curses for future generations to have a better quality of life. Although we are physically free, there's still a slavery mentality pertaining to wealth and money that must shift. African Americans are the #1 consumers, yet as a culture, we are last on the list when it comes to wealth, and our dollar circulates the least number of times in our own culture and communities. Which means we support other cultures' businesses more than our own WHY? With the rise of racial tension, this has become more of a focus in the past few years, but we still have a long way to go.

In our communities, bankruptcy is pushed as the answer to our money prayers, high-interest payday loans are advertised as a quick solution, and over-drafting your bank account is accepted as the expected standard. Quick credit fixes are the main thing promoted instead of providing more education on credit and helping to truly understand credit to maintain it for a lifetime. Unfortunately, we live in a world of quick fixes instead of real change, changed mindsets, habits, and overall behaviors. I hope you understand that it's okay to make money. It's okay to talk about money. It's okay to be rich. It's okay to have an overflow, and it's okay to reap the harvest and invest in yourself.

Changing Your Mindset

You must first change your thoughts to change your life and your current money situation. It is more complicated than it sounds, but it is possible. I have coached people over the years and have watched them change their situations over time. So how do you change your thoughts? By becoming aware of the thoughts that don't serve your desired outcome. Example: You want to save money for the desired goal, but you notice after reviewing your bank statements that you spend $500 monthly on eating out. Something happens once you have thought about how much you could save by not eating out so much. You begin to question eating out so much.

Once your thoughts begin to shift, your behavior and habits will soon follow, and accountability helps. Something happens when you raise your awareness and have a higher level of importance on something you really want for your life. For example, you will begin to pay closer attention to how much you eat out and how much you spend. You will make better choices like finding discounts on food or cooking. You will notice that saving an additional $500 a month becomes extremely important. Once you set a goal in your mind and you shift your perspective, you can achieve anything.

After your thoughts have shifted and your behavior begins to change, your new money habits will start to form. We tend to do many things based on the habits we have developed backed by our belief system. Whether these habits were taught intentionally, or we learned them along the way, from our parents or whoever, the brain doesn't know the difference. It is said that once you have a new habit for 21 days, it becomes a part of your routine. Good money habits like sticking to a budget, understanding your credit, saving money consistently, and being aware of your debt to income are all good money habits and require your dedicated focus.

Values and Beliefs

Your values and beliefs control your entire life. Understanding your values and belief system is extremely important to know and understand. Untimely values and beliefs control your money mindset. You don't value things in your life by accident. Your values influence what is most important in your life. It's how you measure standards and character, loyalty, and respect. Chasing money should never cost you your soul. Everything should be put into proper perspective. Which Means God, family, joy, peace, and your personal value system should all come before money. You decide what is essential to you every day, and you determine that based on your thoughts, habits, and behaviors. If you value a new pair of shoes overpaying your bills, it's because you believe those shoes are essential. For example, I love work-life balance, autonomy, and family/friend relationships. At the end of the day, I have to place this thing on a high level of focus to match my value system. It is also essential to understand that your values can change over time, and you get to choose what you value the most.

Your beliefs are a little bit different. Our beliefs are what we believe to be accurate; We have a conviction of existence even without proof. Beliefs impact your morals, lying, cheating, etc. Beliefs are primarily about religion, but I would like to challenge your thinking regarding values and beliefs. There are many ways to make money, some people earn it, and some do illegal activities. I am not judging anyone's income source, but I challenge people to consider their moral compass when making money. At the end of your life, you can't take money with you. Also, understand that we have been given instructions when it comes to valuing money over God and not respecting your values and beliefs.

Chapter 2

Principles of A Poverty Mindset

"How long will you lay there, you lazy person? When will you get up from sleeping?"
(Proverbs 6:9, NCV)

"Poverty is a disease of the mind"
S. B. Fuller

Let's Talk About Lack

There are two types of mindsets you have related to money. The first one is a poverty mindset. A poverty mindset is a lack-based mindset. You always feel like there is never enough. Even when you have money, you are always saying you are broke. This type of mindset keeps you always looking for a handout and thinking someone owes you something. "Poverty, on the other hand, is undesirable and unnecessary. Misery, debt, and lack directly result from poverty consciousness and victim psychology that springs from thoughts of limitation and fear. It is a form of living hell caused by man's blindness. To end the unlimited opportunities and abundance plays before him." Kimbro, Dennis, et al. "1." Think and Grow Rich: A Black Choice, Fawcett Columbine, New York, New York, 1997, pp. 43.

People with this type of mindset never seem to want better for themselves, or at least they don't take action to make things better for themselves. Poverty-minded people sometimes think they are not worthy of wealth and abundance and tend to sabotage opportunities and get in their own way of wealth or growth. A poverty-minded person can never seem to get ahead in life. They tend to live paycheck to paycheck and live well above their means. They live for the moment, overspend to keep up with other people, and never consider the future. People with a poverty mindset stay at jobs they really want to leave until they frustrate themselves instead of finding a better job or starting a business. Then, they remain in that old job too long out of fear of a better opportunity.

As a faith-based community, do we think it's normal to serve God yet be lacking, struggling, and broke?

These conditions contradict everything God has told us and everything he teaches us in His word. Why do we accept a mindset and a mind-frame of not having enough as okay? When God already told us that we are wealthy, we just have to go after it. It's time to shift the trajectory of our lives and our families' lives. I have seen so many faith-based people who should have more and live abundant lives than others in the world, yet that's not the case. So many times, in my coaching, I often see people want the best God has for them and are excited for what's coming, but they don't do the natural work needed to bring financial blessings into their lives. God is not a genie! He's not somebody that magically comes and changes our lives. God creates trees and plants, not tables and chairs. He provides the resources, but He needs us to put in the work to make something wonderful. There is work needed to be done on our part. Now, He will bless anything we touch, but faith without works is dead. So, it's time for us to start putting our hands on some things. It's time to start putting some things in place. The minute things are in place is the minute we write the book, write the play, start the business, and go after the things and the dreams, visions, desires, promises, and purposes of God.

It is the minute that our life changes forever, and we will be financially blessed.

We may not see everything unfold in a single moment, but you will notice small changes as time goes on. Something happens in the spirit realm when we decide to change our minds. A powerful decision pulls on the anointing, and the shift happens. Favor falls on us because we decided to act on a gift and passion that God has put on inside of us. So we won't live and stay in the same place long. We won't stay in the wilderness when we've already been promised the promised land. It's time for us to go forward and change our mindset. Even when we have Giants to fight, we must know we already have the victory. Changing your mindset is not easy, but you can choose to start today. It's time for us to change our lives and go after the things we desire. We can't go backward. Slavery is a thing of the past, and a better future is on the other side of the hard work. We can't stay where we are, right now, in limbo. The only thing left to do is move forward to go after everything God's already promised us.

Suppose this is the time to change your mindset now. It's never too late to change your situation, and the first step is realizing a change is needed and that you deserve better. The first step is to face your reality. The next step is to learn how you speak to yourself. Words and thoughts have power. The power of life and death is in your tongue. So what are you telling yourself about your money situation?

Are you speaking and thinking life or death when it comes to your life and finances?

Overcoming Limiting Beliefs

Believe it or not, you can have limiting beliefs when it comes to money. You can sabotage your future when it comes to having more money, building businesses, and taking on new jobs when it comes to receiving an increase. Sometimes, you sabotage your financial future when you have a mindset that hasn't completely shifted to everything God has for you. I've done this before; I have held myself back because I didn't think I deserved the increase. In fact, I've had so many revelations while writing this book. In a way, in some parts of this book, I am literary writing to myself as I prepare for this next level. Even though I've been financial savvy for a long time, I also helped coach people through situations and worked in banking and finance for several years. There are still some shifts in my mindset that had to happen to take me from where I am now to where I'm going next.

There's always a level of elevation that comes with God positioning you into excellence. Sometimes whether that's taking a new job opportunity with more money than you ever made in your life or even building a new business, growth requires a new version of yourself that you may not have even met yet. Do you want a new job or want to start a business? Any financial shift also requires you to think about money differently. It requires you to think about how you receive money differently. It requires you to think about what you will put your hands to next and become responsible. God is going to bless you, but what are you going to put your hands to? The biggest challenge is when you don't grow up with money, and then suddenly, you continuously have elevation. You get to a pivotal place where you know the decisions and choices you're making will not only change your own life. They're going to change somebody else life. What decision can you make today about money that can change your children's lives? Now, that's a scary feeling. It's so frightening and challenging that it requires a different version of yourself and your mind to elevate.

Sometimes those limiting beliefs start to kick in to tell you that you can't do it, that nobody ever did it before, that you're going to fail, that you will always be poor, and that you will never have enough money. You can even start talking yourself out of your blessings. You start thinking that you have all these things going on with you when it's just your mind shifting to a whole new level. It does require a different, higher version of you. So when you start to think about plans and position yourself to take yourself to a whole new level of receiving money as you've never had before. It can be both scary and exciting. I would start recognizing when you feel those feelings and think those thoughts. Notice, sometimes it's the devil talking to you that's trying to talk you out of the abundance and wealth because he doesn't want you to succeed. You have to decide on truth, and only God's word is truth. So as you begin to expand and rebuke those limiting mindsets and beliefs, know that the best version of your life is coming. How bad do you want it?

Chapter 3

Principles of An Abundance Mindset

"With God's power working in us, God can do much more than anything we can ask or imagine." (Ephesians 3:20, NCV)

Abundance is the second types of mindset related to money. Now I have to say this! True abundance, wealth, and prosperity are not all about money. You can have abundance in your relationships, be wealthy in resources, and live a happy, prosperous life without being rich from a money standpoint. You can also value things so much that they are priceless in your eyes. For example, my grandfather was not wealthy when it came to money, but he was rich in knowledge and love. I learned so much from him by sitting at the table and talking to him for hours. He could make you laugh about anything and had a contagious smile, pure joy. He lived to be 98 years old, which is a wisdom that you can't buy anywhere and can never be replaced. A person with an abundance mindset looks at a world full of hope and new opportunities. They constantly seek knowledge and understand God's promises for them. They are excited about the future and look for multiple ways to gain wealth. They tend to be aware of their finances and is a giver. A person with an abundance mindset plans for the future and wants to leave generational wealth. They don't compare their financial situations with others because they know what God has for them is for them. They utilize a budget and live below their means. They practice good stewardship over everything they manage on this earth. They consistently see growth and blessings in multiple areas of their life. "prosperity is the result of correct thoughts, inactive way of thinking and living in accordance with spiritual principles." Kimbro, Dennis, et al. "1." Think and Grow

Rich: A Black Choice, Fawcett Columbine, New York, New York, 1997, pp. 43.

Abundance and Overflow

It's beautiful to know that we can have God's best for us. Speak life into your money situation every day from this point on. You deserve wealth, prosperity, and abundance as your birthright. The sooner you come to this understanding, the sooner you will reach an abundance mindset. Everything may not show up overnight. You will have to do the work to get the outcome you desire. One of the first steps is realizing you need help and taking action for a better future. It's time for you to have more than enough so you can help other people have more.

Having money is good. It's okay to have money! I will say that again; It's okay to have money. It is okay to have overflow. It's okay to be wealthy. Release yourself from any bondage in this area so your actions don't hold you back. I know several people that have struggled in this area. I have also struggled with accepting money, charging the correct prices, and asking for raises because a part of me felt unworthy. This mindset shift has to happen for you to have money long-term. It is not easy, but it is worth it. Become comfortable talking about money. When people give you money, say thank you and don't talk them out of their blessing. When you notice that funny feeling that comes up that makes you feel uncomfortable, recognize it, and think positive thoughts. Eventually, this gets easier.

Now it is time to determine what type of mindset you have. These two mindsets determine how you approach your thinking, make money, and spend money. The two mindsets even determine how you handle financial situations that happen in your life. Your mindset is determined based on several factors, your thoughts, behaviors, habits, values, and beliefs.

Abundance is your birthright. You are entitled to the very things that God has for you. And money is no different. He already offers you wealth. He already provides you with more than enough. He already gives to you exceedingly and abundantly. But the reality of it is we are not always connected. So that means sometimes, we shift our mindset to a place where it does not belong. Money is free to give money; it's simply energy, and it flows to us with ease and grace when we open ourselves to be able to receive it and give it away.

What would happen if you opened up your mind to be able to receive everything God has for you? What would happen if you saw every day as a new opportunity to acquire wealth and overflow in your life? What would happen if you completely shifted yourself to be able to be a shear magnet for money and wealth in your life? What would happen if that possibility were a reality? Who would you be? How would your life be different? How would your family's life be different? It's time to shift and move into the next stage of your life and no longer dread the very things that are not real.

Just Ask

I was hoping you could begin writing down and speaking the things you want. If you need a certain amount of money for something, I want you to start to ask for it. I know that we serve an almighty God, so asking him for $10, like what's $10? When you can ask Him for $100,000. We can even ask Him for a million. Start testing the waters and writing down what a million dollars looks like for you in a journal or a notebook. What would you do with one million dollars? What would you do with a billion dollars? We always dream so small. We always think, oh, I just need $100 for this bill, or I just need $200 for that bill. Oh, I need enough money just to get gas or food for the day. I just need gas money for the week. Often when we have a limited mindset or just operating in lack, God can only give us a little bit. We talk ourselves out of so much in life. What if we asked for that million, and we saw it happen? What if we asked for a billion, and we see it happen? God will give us the money, or He will give us the resources to obtain the money, talents, skills, and gifts. So, let's start asking for bigger things. Let's begin dreaming on another level to obtain the money God has for us. Let's start committing ourselves to think so abundantly that God doesn't have a choice but to bless us in this next season. So, while I look at where my life is today, I know this book and other things I'm working on now will bless my life. My life is going to be completely different from what it is now. I can already see the complete transformation from what it was ten years ago. The biggest thing that

I'm going to do from this moment on is I'm going to ask bigger. I will begin to ask for items that are out of this world because my father can provide them. We get so limited in our mindset, and we get so little in our thinking that we don't even consider the things that are possible in our lives. So after this moment, start asking for bigger so that you can advance your mind and completely change your life.

Chapter 4

Principles of Your Relationship with Money

"No servant can serve two masters the servant will hate one master and love the other, or will follow one master and refuse to follow the other. You cannot serve both God and worldly riches."

(Luke 16:13, NCV)

Did you realize you even have a relationship with money? Your relationship with money determines your overall quality of life. How you relate to money drives your choices in your life. It determines the type of jobs you take and the promotions you take to make more money. Some people love money and are willing to sacrifice their entire life chasing it. They tend to put money above anything and everyone, even God. Some people are afraid of having a lot of money for fear that they will change. Some people get nervous when they are in the presence of a lot of money.

Your Feelings and Your Money

Let's face reality. God is the source. Money is simply a resource. The sooner we can understand this concept, put God first, and allow him into the situation, the more we will receive. But for some reason, we feel guilty for wanting more. We feel ashamed that we don't have it. And we feel bitter or angry when others have money and we don't. Everyone didn't always have the opportunity to have money. We, as African Americans, come from descendants of slaves, so wealth was not something we continue to see or know in our bloodline. We've had to put the pieces together of our lives and find ways to make it. And so the reality is that some things just don't feel comfortable. But it's time that we start to get comfortable with money. Even though we didn't see wealth, we only saw hard work. It's time for us to change. The reality of what we see is that our families don't want to talk about money. Well, it's time for us to change that. We didn't have money, nor did we share or have these things in conversation. Everything was private. It's not taught in schools. It's not taught in churches, but it's time for us to fill the gaps. We will no longer feel shame and guilt about money and not investing in ourselves. We work hard to have everything we ever wanted in life. It's okay to save and no longer live in fear.

Get out of feelings because it is impacting your money.

Ask yourself these questions and write down your answers.

How do you feel when you think about money?

Are you happy and excited? Are you mad and upset? Are you worried or anxious?

Emotional Spending

Do you notice how your feelings change when you have money and when you don't? Do you realize when your feelings shift your mood?

What would you be telling money if it was a person? Have you ever stopped talking to the very thing you use daily? What would you say?

Often times you can have painful emotions around money that you may need to heal. Look back over your life. Do you remember times when you or your parents couldn't afford something which brought you pain or anxiety? I remember times in my life when I was a little girl when my mom was not present for important events at school because she had to work to make money. As a single mother of three, she raised us the best she could, but it was defiantly not always easy. Growing up, I remember times we couldn't afford lights or heat. These were my first thoughts about money and setting priorities in life. We often experience things as young children that we don't fully understand, but we remember the pain of being upset or disappointed, and then the root cause of the pain was related to money.

We all have feelings when it comes to our money. The reality is that we think and feel some type of way when we have to make money, pay bills, etc. We think about what we want to buy and get upset when we can't purchase certain things. We go to the store and spend money on things that we don't really need when we're upset because we're emotionally spending. We get depressed when we can't buy gifts, or we can't buy certain things we feel like we want. We get overwhelmed when it comes time to think about paying for vacations and something that should be exciting, but we get stressed out over the amount of money it costs. The truth is, we all have feelings when it comes to money. That thing on the inside of you makes you feel a certain way. You can feel the energy in your mind and body shift whenever you think about paying for something that costs a lot, or paying fines, etc., especially if you don't have the money. Your feelings may be much stronger if you grew up without the money. Especially when you don't think you're going to make money or even when you lose money altogether.

Behavior

Have you ever lost a large amount of money before or had to pay for something that you didn't have the money to pay for at the time? An overwhelming feeling takes over your body and controls and shifts your energy. Have you ever sat and really thought about how you feel about money? Like what emotions you tie to certain things because it drives the outcome of that situation and the result of your money experience. Do you ever feel dread when you have to pay for something specific? You should be thankful for paying bills because you had the money to pay them. Some people can't pay bills at all. Frequently we say we hate paying this bill, or I'm tired of paying for this debt, but do you know what it feels like to be unable to pay for something at all? You should consider and connect to how you feel about money at this point in your life. Sit back and be thankful for the money you have to pay for things. Be excited about new opportunities and new money that's coming your way and be grateful that you can get up and do it all over again. Once you heal your feelings, you will also heal your soul, and you can change your habits and behavior. It's definitely worth the work!

"Your heart will be where your treasure is." (Luke 12:34)

Forgiveness

How do you feel about your finances??

If you're at the end of this chapter, and we've talked about your feelings and your relationship with money, more than likely, you will realize that you've had some negative thoughts and feelings about money. You may remember sometimes you didn't have it or growing up struggling. No one is perfect at handling money or excellent at handling everything. We all learn from experiences, right? So you've had your experiences and your situations up till now. And hopefully, after reading this book, you'll have a different perspective on your mindset and your feelings that you may need to change and do differently. But before you can even go into the next section of this book, I want you to sit for a moment and forgive yourself. I want you to forgive yourself for your past thoughts and negative energy towards money and shift your perspective more positively.

Once you forgive money, commit to creating a better relationship with your money. These next steps require some additional action and some additional self-reflection. But you can only go deeper into these things if you have offered forgiveness and go into it with a grateful heart because it's hard to put additional energy and effort into something you don't want to do. You still have negative feelings coming up. So I need you to have an open mind. I also need You to forgive and move forward. I look forward to helping you to the next part of this journey.

Chapter 5

Principles of Budgeting Basics

"Write down the vision; write it clearly on clay tablets so whoever reads it can run to tell others."
(Habakkuk 2:2, NCV)

Why do you need a budget?

Your budget is your guide, a form of a vision for your finances. You cannot be successful with money when you are operating blindly.

Creating Your Budget

Just keep it simple. Now, many people will tell you a lot of different ways that you can make a budget. And there are a lot of other options. You can write everything down. You can utilize different apps on your phone. You can utilize Excel spreadsheets. Whatever works for you is what I suggest. When I consult with customers, I have them start with an Excel spreadsheet first, but that's only for me to see and understand where they are, save a copy, and track their progress. But for you daily, you have to use what's most comfortable for you. Something that you will regularly maintain, an Excel spreadsheet may not work for everybody. So here's what I say: try each of them and figure out what feels more comfortable. I am more of a "write things down" type of person. I prefer using a pencil and a book. I like actual budget books or planners. I prefer to see it, touch it feel it. I prefer to write everything down. It helps me connect; connecting helps me to commit things to memory. However, each person is different, and there's no right or wrong way to track your budget as long as you have all your expenses and income included. Just do the budget.

It can be more challenging if you're just starting out utilizing a budget, but it gets easier over time. If you're just trying to figure out a place to start and want the first step, just start by simply tracking your income every month by reviewing your bank statements and your monthly expenses. How much money is coming in, and how much is going out. Every time you purchase something or pay a bill, just write it down. You could carry around a little book or a notepad to help you. You can also use your phone, whatever you feel most comfortable using. A good tip is to keep all your receipts or take pictures of them each day and write down everything from the entire day when you get home. The goal is for you to simply track your income minus your expenses over time. In about 30 to 60 days, you'll see a better picture of where your money goes each month. Once you start consistently using your budget, you will know where you can cut expenses, reduce spending, and understand the full scope of your finances. Once you do your budget a few times, it gets easier.

For some reason, many people hate to write down a budget. They say it feels like it's restrictive. They have created the mindset that it hinders them instead of helping them. Another issue is they tend to feel like they don't have enough money when they are done. So why should they do a budget? The truth is a budget is there to help you. It is there to give you a month-to-month guide. It's there to help you see things you may not be able to see or understand without calculating the numbers for yourself. It helps you set your financial goals and determine what you need to do next. A budget is actually freedom. It gives you the freedom to know where you are, setting up goals and things to get to where you are in the short term and where you want to be long term. It also helps you keep track of any kind of overspending. It enables you to keep track of your debt. It also lets you track what you spend your money on monthly.

People are often resistant to a budget because they don't want to know where their money is going, or they don't know how to do one correctly. We all know when we have trouble with eating out or buying clothes. We all know someone that loves buying shoes, hair products, or shopping on QVC or Amazon. Whatever you love, shoes, clothes, food, etc., it's okay. We all have trouble in certain areas of our life. Your goal is to budget for these things so that you don't overspend. Your budget is there to help you with the things you need and the things that you want. And NO, tracking your transactions online or from your phone is different from creating a budget.

Preparing your budget is really to help you with setting goals. What are your top three goals? Keep it very simple whenever you're setting these up. List goals that you can achieve within the next three to six months, maybe within the next 90 days even, and expand to plans within the next three years, but you want to set up those financial goals that you have for yourself and your budget, so it helps you stay on track. Whether it's paying off debt, creating a savings plan, adjusting your lifestyle, or planning for a different lifestyle, keep it realistic to your situation. You can even plan for your vacations. You literally could plan for anything and everything. If you want to go on vacation, say in June, and you start planning in January, you have six months to prepare for that particular vacation. That means you can save so much each month, and you're not trying to spend all of your June paycheck paying for this vacation. You can plan for Christmas the same way. We all know it comes every single year at the same time. We should not be going into debt or spending bill money to purchase gifts for Christmas. You can have a specific account you are putting Christmas money into where you can save so much money every month.

Maybe you're saving $100 a month or $50 a month. You should have your entire Christmas fund saved up overtime at the end of the year. Instead, I often see people spend their December paycheck on Christmas, go into debt, utilize credit cards to pay for Christmas, and struggle in January, February, and March. Usually, they struggle until about tax season, have to re-adjust their lifestyles, and do it again the following year. So having a budget helps you stay consistent and know your goals and what you're working towards. Keep your savings plan at the top of your mind. I'm not saying you will be perfect because nobody is perfect. But, awareness, self-reflection, and understanding of your goals will help you now. You may need other things, like accountability, additional help, resources, and support. You at least need to be connected to your situation. Because at the end of the day, this impacts your entire life.

Once you've outlined and tracked your expenses and income, the next thing is for you to identify any spending habits that need to change. So everybody has a money habit that needs to change. Whether you like to eat at McDonald's every day, enjoy nice shoes, love purses, earrings, or jewelry, it doesn't matter what item you have a spending habit on; everybody has a habit. For example, you may realize you always pay a bill late or just have to purchase something the very day you get paid. It's challenging to even change your spending habit sometimes but having that revelation that I need to change this area is necessary. You have a budget that outlines your spending habits, but you want to first know what that looks like for you and your lifestyle. Where does your money go? Do you have frivolous spending habits? Do you have emotional-based spending habits? Knowing what you're paying and spending your money on helps you change and shift anything. It enables you to understand your patterns. It allows you to understand yourself as a person. You may even think, hey, I need to change this.

Keeping a budget will reveal if you're eating or drinking someplace expensive and spending a good bit of money each month. You may even realize what you're eating is not even healthy for you. So it helps you also understand your lifestyle where you may need to make changes. Does it align with your health and fitness goals? Can you cut back? Does it align with your overall goals of wanting to purchase stocks, mutual funds, or invest in your 401(k) a little more? So knowing where you are spending your money is crucial. It's vital to save and critical to shift your habits and behaviors. So, setting that up and connecting to your habits will help you identify your spending habits journey.

The key to any budget is just being honest with yourself, sitting down, and being honest with yourself about the money you're spending and receiving. When working with clients, I find they often don't want to face reality, so they ignore it. They know they're spending money in places they don't need to but are unsure how to change. Often, people run from what feels uncomfortable and situations they don't know how to fix. They also know they may not have enough to pay their bills. They just haven't reasonably identified what the issue is. I often noticed that because we don't know what the problem is, we continue doing the same thing repeatedly instead of stopping and outlining why something is not working. When I went through financial hardship and faced foreclosure at one point, I had to sit down and be honest with myself after my divorce. When I did my monthly budget, I was in the red, so I didn't have enough income to support my expenses. When I wrote out my budget, my income was half of my monthly expenses. So that was a reality check for me. I had to learn how to control my expenses. If not, If I continued down the road, I was on with only half of what I needed to cover bills every month, I would worsen my financial situation. Now I can say that God always provides in those situations in those months of struggling and making changes. While navigating through a divorce and trying to adjust my bills, I had to plan differently, to survive and plan for a better financial future. Many things shifted for me, but I can say that God always provided, and He always showed up on time. I was never without lights. I was never without food. Although I didn't have everything I always wanted and had to sell some things like TVs and other electronics, I had more than I needed. Many opportunities came from my struggling to improve my financial situation, it was difficult, but I can talk and speak about it now to help others have hope in moving forward. Sometimes you realize who you are and how strong you are in the struggle, but if you don't face your situation and don't realize where you need help, you can't change anything. I have learned that God allowed some things to happen to me to test my faith and keep me focused on Him and not this world.

Ways to Budget

A fantastic way to create a budget is using the 50, 30, 20 rule. With this rule, 50% of your income goes towards your monthly living expenses. 30% goes towards your lifestyle expenses, and 20% goes towards saving for your future. Realistically everybody only has 100%, right? For example, if it's $1,000, if it's $5,000, if it's $10,000. You only have 100% coming in every month. So where are you spending your money? How are you dividing up what you make? You should not spend everything in one place, or at least that's not the best lifestyle to have.

You can't save everything because then how are you going to live and how are you going to eat but you also can't spend it all on your lifestyle, shopping, eating out and things like that. The most ideal budget is to divide it up where it makes sense for you and your expenses. You can also change your percentages, but the goal is 50, 30, and 20. This is the best outline because it gives you a nice balance to your money. Sometimes you may be in a season where 60% of your income goes towards living expenses. You have to figure out how you want to allocate that additional debt additional 40% I would say, you know, to make the 50, 30, 20 your goal, but if you're not there when you add out your bills, make sure you're connected to what that looks like for you so you can change it. The other thing is that the 50, 30, and 20 rule helps you stay on track with living below your means regarding your expenses. If you're at 50% utilization on your living expenses, you're in a better situation where you can cut lifestyle expenses. You can even cut saving towards the future even though it's not the best practice, and you want to ensure you're saving for your future. If anything happens, you're living off half of your income. This is great as you continue to increase your revenue and not consume more debt. This keeps you in a mode or a mentality to always be mindful of where you're spending your money, and you will gradually see your money increase.

You should be updating and utilizing your budget monthly. Every month before you sit down and pay anything, you should make sure you have a budget outlined on what you're paying, what date you're paying it, and how much you need to pay. You should update this every month because things may change, right? Some expenses are fixed, meaning they don't change like your car note, but some expenses are variable, meaning they change month to month like your electric bill. You must prepare for the unexpected. Last month, your gas and electric bill might have been $100. This month your electric bill might be $200. You need to adjust your budget and prepare for that difference of $100 more. If you don't budget correctly, you will live paycheck to paycheck. Don't worry about feeling restrictive because a budget is not there to restrict you. In this electric bill scenario, you will be able to plan for the increase of $100. Your budget is there to give you a vision and help set goals. It's also there to guide you on what you need to do and how things may work out.

The other thing I will suggest is to reward yourself monthly. Sometimes, it's complicated. I know we're talking about money, and I know sometimes it sounds like we as coaches are always saying, "Don't spend money." I always have my clients create a section of how much they will spend on the things they love to do, eat, or purchase. I notice what happens if we continue to starve ourselves from everything. That's when we go off track because we feel like we can't have anything. It's almost like being on a diet and saying that even though you love sweets, you can't have any sugar or don't eat any sweets ever again. Over time, you will binge eat because you can only do that for so long. Then, when you go back to sugar, you almost overeat and want all the sugar because you've been depriving yourself for so long. What we want to see with your money habits is a consistent lifestyle change. Your budget, your money habits, and your behaviors can work similarly. You want to stay connected to where your money is going monthly, but you also want to reward yourself for staying on track. Having a budget doesn't mean you can't buy things you love. In most situations, you just have to be more aware of how you spend your money. You need to know where your money is being spent to ensure your expenses are paid first. Then, you can change or alter it to ensure you're staying on track at any time.

Creating a reasonable budget that identifies the lowest amount you can spend each month helps reduce your spending on paper, reduces your payments to only debt, and helps preserve income is ideal. Create a worst-case scenario plan after you reduce your income that reveals impacts to family etc. Prepare to invest and build up your skill set, stop significant spending and educate yourself to become a good steward of your money. Your budget is your blueprint, and you can't master what you can't manage. Create new wealth habits for yourself. Reduce expenses. There's an enormous difference between needs and wants. Become consistent, identify unhealthy spending habits, and make a plan to change. "A better budget is built from the brick of facts and figures about your finances:

A very specific and accurate understanding of how much you bring in every month." Aliche, Tiffany. "2." Get Good with Money: Ten Simple Steps to Becoming Financially Whole, Harmony Books, New York, NY, 2021, p. 30.

Chapter 6

Principles of Credit Basics

"And patience produces character,
and character produces hope."
(Romans 5:4, NCV)

Credit Reflection

Okay, it's time to get your credit together. When it comes to your credit, just breathe and be patient. I know this is one of the more difficult things to discuss. I have noticed over the years that discussing our credit score can come with a lot of shame and guilt, depending on where you are in your credit journey. It's a lot of the ins and outs when it comes to credit. You are not alone if you feel that understanding your credit is confusing. This is the main topic that people always say during my coaching session. "I wish I had known that before now." I know we don't learn about credit soon enough, and we tend to start learning about credit when we need it, like when we want to buy a house or rent an apartment. You can get into trouble very quickly at a young age, and it is easy to do when you don't watch your credit or don't realize how your credit impacts your life. Credit can dictate your path the most out of everything related to your finances. Credit dictates job opportunities, your ability to get home loans, and your interest rates on cars and other loans. There are a lot of factors that go into you being consistently responsible when it comes to your credit. So if you're at a place where you're trying to get better with your credit, we will offer you some tips and know that improving your credit is not an overnight quick fix. You didn't get into trouble with your credit overnight, and it does take more than a couple of letters to fix all your credit issues.

I know some people will tell you to do a credit repair agency, and those things are fine for the moment. However, if you never truly learned about credit or don't understand everything that goes into having good credit, how can you maintain it long-term? Some things might fix your credit and give you an excellent score for the moment to get one thing. Still, if you never review your credit report, learn life lessons, and understand how things impact your credit score daily, you're likely to get back into the same situation you were once in.

Your credit is essential for multiple reasons, but the number one reason is that it reflects your overall responsibility. Creditors want to know that you're dependable enough to repay them if they decide to lend you money. Your score reflects that if you borrow money from them, you will pay it back on time monthly and satisfy the debt in full. Overall, that's what your credit score represents, and some factors are used to determine your score, which we will cover in this chapter. The better you are at adhering to all the credit factors and remaining responsible month after month, the higher your credit score. You are viewed as more trustworthy with good credit, and creditors believe you will promptly pay back the money you borrow. On the other hand, bad credit makes you look like a risk to lenders, and they tend to think they may not get their money back from you, so they deny credit or give you a higher interest rate.

Jobs and Credit

Credit can impact job opportunities and even the ability to obtain new credit, expanding your business. Sometimes companies pull your credit report because they want to know what type of person you are based on your credit history. Just like above, they want to see if you're responsible. If you are ensuring that you satisfy any debt that you owe. Your credit file paints a picture of the type of individual they may be hiring. So you want to ensure that you keep an eye on your credit and the kind of things reported on your credit report because your credit report can determine if you are selected for a job, not just for loans, etc.

Benefits of Good Credit

There are several benefits to good credit. So the main benefit of having good credit is paying lower interest rates on loans. So, for example, if you want to purchase a car and have good credit, you tend to get 3% interest rates or maybe even a 0% interest rate if you have exceptional credit on that entire car loan debt. Paying a max of 3%, which is suitable for an interest rate on a car loan for $20,000 with no down payment for, let us just say, five years, would cost you $21,562.43, So you would pay $1,562.43 in interest over five years. If your interest rate was 0%, you would not pay any interest, and the cost would only be the original $20,000. Compared to somebody with a lower credit score, they will end up paying more. This example was just on a car note, but somebody may pay ten times on a debt over a lifetime, depending on their credit score. Please note that you can also have more negotiation power with good credit.

Another benefit to good credit is the ability to obtain new credit quickly. Creditors consider you a good bet or lower risk when you already have good credit. When you take new credit, as long as your debt-to-income ratio is good, they'll offer you new credit, and you'll have better opportunities to get it across different companies. Depending on what you're purchasing, a creditor may run your credit, and only one or two creditors may accept you and offer you new credit. When you have good credit, all of them will accept you, and you can determine the best options for your situation to have a better deal long term. The greatest thing about having good credit is having more options for what you're trying to do in life.

Impacts of Poor Credit

There are several impacts to having poor credit that can cost you so much money over a lifetime. Similar to the example above, but in reverse, you can purchase a car, but they will still let you buy the vehicle if you have poor credit. However, your interest rate may be more than 15%- 20%, and you're paying a 20% interest rate which makes your monthly payments higher. So if we take that same $20,000 for five years at a 20% interest, you will pay $11,793 over five years. Having poor credit increases the total money you'll pay to that creditor over time. So where someone with good credit may pay 0% and 3%.

Because of their credit, someone with bad credit could pay up to 20%, which is almost ten times more money for the exact same vehicle and the same loan term.

Another impact of having poor credit is stress. You tend to be more stressed or anxious when unsure how you will pay for something you need or want. When you need a car, when you want a home for your family, when you really need a loan for whatever reason, and you can't seem to be able to get money, it does not feel good. It is stressful to have people pull your credit when you know it is not good. You already know they are looking at your credit to determine how responsible you are, but you already know you have not taken this seriously. It can be extremely stressful when you want something and try to do something to better your situation, yet you just can't get it. This level of stress can increase health issues and have an overall negative impact on your health. You end up looking at situations, and you're unsure how you will get out of your current situation. Have you ever experienced all the phone calls from creditors for late or charged-off bills? It's many downstream impacts to not having the money. Some people may say to live a cash-only life, but no credit is the same as poor credit. As you move on to obtain new things having credit helps you build when you don't have cash on hand. There is a difference between having debt which is more of a liability, and funding, which is an asset.

Another impact of poor credit is being denied new credit. So you may have situations where you want to purchase a home or a car, but you're denied because when they pull your credit score, you are considered a risk. They're not willing to take that risk on you with your credit score being so low. The biggest thing is your responsibility for credit, and you cannot get the things you need. When you are denied, you can feel less than or unworthy. Although I have seen and heard several reasons why someone has poor credit, you can always work on it and make changes to your situation. With good credit, the lender looks at your history and trusts that you'll likely pay back what you owe timely.

On the other hand, bad credit means that you are more likely to be more of a risk to the lender. Perhaps you have not paid loans back or not paid them back on time. Any collections will also impact your score and your creditworthiness. As you learn more, don't take this credit process personally. "Even though we use the term good and bad when talking about credit, none of this is a judgment on goodness or badness of you as a person." Aliche, Tiffany. "5" Get Good with Money: Ten Simple Steps to Becoming Financially Whole, Harmony Books, New York, NY, 2021, p. 115.

Another thing you want to make sure that you do concerning your credit is check your credit score regularly. You are entitled to at least one free credit report a year. You can also get more free credit reports with the right memberships and credit support connections. You have no idea how often people put errors on your credit report. Things can be removed or updated that are simple to increase your score, but instead, these items reduce your credit score. Sometimes creditors can put inaccurate information on your credit report, and you can dispute it. You also want to make sure you're connected to your credit score. So if it shifts or changes, you know what that might be. So you want to ensure that your information is correct on your credit report. So again, it's a good practice to manage your credit that you overlook and that you continue to stay connected to your credit.

Another important thing is a credit monitoring service that monitors your bank accounts and personal information and protects you against fraud. In case you ever become a victim of identity theft. Monitoring services can keep track of your bank accounts, email addresses, and phone numbers, so your personal information will be tracked, which is very good today. So when you get to the point of having good credit, keep track of the things that helped you maintain your credit by reducing any issues or inaccuracies on your report.

Credit information

Your credit score has five different ratings: poor, fair, good, very good, and exceptional. Poor is 300 to 580, fair is 580 to 669, good is 670 to 739, very good is 742 to 799, and exceptional is 800 to 850. Equifax, Experian, and Trans Union are the three industries that report your credit information. The most common terms are credit report, credit score, and the credit bureau. Your credit information and calculated credit score are divided into five categories. Payment History at 35%, amounts at 30%, inquiries at 10%, length of credit history at 15%, and a mixture of credit is 10%. If you have multiple types of credit, meaning installment loans, credit cards, and a mortgage, you have numerous types of credit that increase your score. Your goal for your credit score should be at least 740, which is good. Focus on maintaining or improving this score if you are there. Soft credit inquiries do not require permission and do not impact your score. They only pull partial information. Hard inquiries require permission, impact your score, and require your social security number. If you utilize your credit card, you should stay under at least a 30- 40% utilization because that impacts your credit score if you go above that 30-40% of your available credit. Please also ensure you pay your bills on time or early.

Journey

Now my journey with credit repair began when I went through my divorce. During that experience, I struggled to shift my budget and reduce my bills. I found myself needing to pay mainly for my needs, which meant I mostly spent my money on what I needed to pay to survive. Then I found myself with a 530 credit score which is considered poor credit. I had to rebuild my credit piece by piece. My rebuild journey to an excellent status didn't happen overnight, but I was able to gradually elevate my credit score over time. I have learned steps to both rebuild and maintain excellent credit. Please know doing this right is a learning journey, and although I have rebuilt my credit, I still remember how it feels to have poor credit. I remember the internal shame of my situation and how it felt every time I was denied credit. Repairing my credit score was one thing but healing my mind was completely different. As you begin to improve your credit, release any shame or guilt. Renew your mindset, this is a new journey, and you got this!

Chapter 7

Principles of Stewardship

"Whoever can be trusted with a little can also be trusted with a lot, and whoever is dishonest with a little is dishonest with a lot."
(Luke 16:10, NCV)

Good Stewardship

For God to trust you with a lot, He has to know he can trust you with a little. You have to learn to be responsible with your money; being responsible doesn't happen overnight. Some situations occur in life that may impact how we manage money and how we learn about money. You should not be wasteful with anything God gives you because then, why should he give you more? When you finish your budget and understand your spending habits and behaviors, simply ask yourself, "Are there areas where I am wasteful and can be more responsible with God's resources?"

Stay consistent when managing your bills and bank account. It is a good best practice to review your bank account regularly. I've seen many times where customers didn't know how much they were paying for subscription services out of their account. They didn't even know they were being overcharged or double charged because they did not review their bank statements. Sometimes people make mistakes, which can be discovered by studying all your statements.

Nowadays where everything is done electronically, sometimes there are system errors. When you review your bank account regularly and line it up with your budget, it helps you stay on track. Having a plan keeps you from just going in and seeing how much money you have on that day and not accounting for bills that may not have been deducted. The biggest thing is being connected to your account transactions and knowing how much money you have in your account. You should also be connected to the other payments you make from your account and the dates paid.

Managing Expenses

It's essential to learn how to manage your bills. Managing your bills is more than just paying them when you receive them. You want to make sure that you're paying your bills on time every month, not just the ones impacting your credit. Meaning managing credit cards and debt on your credit report and those bills like your gas and electric bill or your cell phone bill that may not be tied to your credit reporting but are still important things that you need to utilize. You want to pay your bills on time to avoid late fees. Number one, late fees are nuisance fees. You don't want to pay additional money on top of what you already owe a company. Number two, It's a waste of money. Number three, you don't have to worry about late fees if you pay bills on time. You don't have to worry about disconnection fees and the stress of having the things you utilize every day being disconnected. So you want to ensure you are constantly paying your bills on time. Being aware of what bills you have, when they are due, and the average amount helps when operating on your budget because this helps you remain consistent, and it also helps you stay on track with paying your bills on time when they're due.

Reducing Bills

Finding ways to reduce your bills is also a good habit when managing your bills. Take a look overall at what you spend your money on once you do your budget, and you can outline everything you are keeping and anything you need to change. Review your spending each month and identify what you can reduce. Often, you can contact companies used for services and see if they have lower packages. Sometimes, they may have lower promotional rates for specific days, services, and subscriptions. Also, make sure you're canceling subscriptions that you don't currently use or don't need anymore. Ask yourself if that subscription aligns with your values and money goals. If you have a subscription service for something like Shoe dazzle and are trying to purchase a house, does that subscription service to purchase additional shoes line up with the ultimate goal? Maybe you're not spending as much, or it may be that you're connected to the costs, and you're okay with it or that it's within your budget. You get to decide, but keep in mind that everybody's goals are different when you have particular goals. You want to ensure those goals and what you're spending money on line up.

Another important thing about managing your bills is how you spend your money. Take a clear look at your budget and understand how you're spending your money. How much is going towards your monthly bills, lifestyle, and your savings? Whichever lifestyle you want, make sure that you know your eating out habit isn't obsessive, or if you're purchasing a lot of things on, say, Amazon or any online network, you're cautious of your spending. You should budget your spending, and you can spend extra money however you like. You just have to make sure that it's within your 100%. Again, everybody only gets 100% to spend every month. So where's your money going? And how are you spending your money consistently to keep track and make sure your regular bills are paid on time and that you're connected to what else you're spending money on?

Here is the reality:

- Thirty-nine percent of Americans cannot even cover a $400 personal emergency.
- Sixty-four percent don't have $1000 saved in the bank.
- Seventy-eight percent of most people live paycheck to paycheck. That's eight out of ten people that you know. If you consider ten people in your circle, eight of them live paycheck to paycheck, and if anything happens to that one source of income, it will completely change their entire lives.

The goal of this book is so that you're not one of those eight people. If you are one of those eight people living paycheck to paycheck right now, let's change that. Take a look at your situation and your circumstance and commit to making a change. So it doesn't completely knock you off your reality. The goal here is to have a better perspective to live a better life. God didn't create us to struggle and not have what we need and want. However, we live in a natural world, so sometimes, things happen beyond our control. Just know no matter your situation, we have supernatural help.

Saving Money

The next category for your savings. Have a retirement account in place. That retirement account could be a mutual fund, or retirement could be your 401(k). That retirement account could even be you dipping into stocks. SAVE SOMETHING. The goal is to have something with higher interest rates or compound interest rates so that you can grow your money quickly. The goal is for you not to have to rely on social security. Also, you're not trying to figure out, once you retire, if you will have enough income to support yourself for the future. Your future is important, and you must plan for it now. So, you shouldn't be spending all of your money now. The reality is you should be able to save at least 20% of your current income for your future to ensure that you're good as you get older. It would help if you also were mindful of other expenses that may come. If you are not saving 20%, start today. If 20% is too much, start with 10%, just begin somewhere.

Emergency Savings

If you want to have an emergency savings account, it needs to have about $1,000 in it for emergencies. This should be an account you can access easily, but it should only be used for emergencies and not to support your spending habit. If something happens like you need a new tire or something quickly for your home, that's an emergency. You should have a savings account on hand with at least $1,000 in it to make sure you can cover quick expenses. The main goal of your emergency savings account is to keep you from going into debt. So many people take out those payday loans or overdraft their accounts when things happen. Try your best to avoid high-interest payday loans or over-drafting your account because these methods are hard to recover from, and you end up in debt pits you can't get out of easily. Your emergency savings should be able to cover some expenses to keep you from going deep into debt. If you don't have this emergency account set up, start one TODAY. If not, you are leaning on credit cards, payday loans, or worse, you cannot cover the emergency at that time, which could negatively impact your daily lifestyle. Please ensure you take this seriously and build on it if needed.

After saving up your emergency account with at least $1000, you also need an expense savings account. And the difference between the two is your expenses savings cover your household bills for an entire month, and you want to have that set up for about six months. If anything happens on your job or in your business or however you primarily receive your income, you know that you have six months' worth of money saved to still pay all your bills for at least the next six months. That temporally alleviates you from having a lot of stress on your life. When you're trying to either find another job or find more ways to increase your income, you know that you have this savings set up just in case. Now, sometimes you may have more significant expenses that may increase. But the biggest thing is to make sure that you have everything set up so you know you're covered. You're not living paycheck to paycheck. You have a nice savings built up.

Insurance

Yes, you should have insurance and keep your policies up to date. You should have insurance on your car to protect it if you're ever involved in an accident. Be sure that your policy covers your vehicle being repaired, replaced, or if an accident is also your fault. You're covered just in case you are liable for another person's injuries. Yes, you should have homeowners' insurance, which protects you if you ever have a fire or damage to your home. If there's stuff involved, any stolen items will also be covered with homeowners' insurance. There are different rounds of renter's insurance that you can investigate to see what the best option is for you. I would also advise that people have life insurance. I feel like this is a topic we don't discuss enough in our culture and community.

We don't talk about death, and we don't talk about what needs to happen when that person dies, whether it is the last will and trust situation, an estate plan, or whether there's life insurance and the coverage, that needs to be taken care of. Life insurance is essential in these scenarios. Even just simply having burial costs saved or prepaid burial plans. Whatever it is, the importance of insurance is for when a person passes away so that the family doesn't have to scrape and scramble to figure out how to cover the funeral cost or debt that that person incurred once that person passes away. So I think this should be a conversation that every household has to make sure they're connected to what the family has established. Whether it's life insurance or pre-burial costs, it needs to be discussed. It needs to be planned out, and it needs to be implemented so that it's not the family trying to grieve and also deal with financial burdens.

I've seen many times where people must start GoFundMe accounts. I've seen people who had to beg for money or get a loan to lay their loved ones to rest. In addition, there may be debt from that loved one that needs to be paid. The family sometimes has to be responsible for the debt and handle all affairs. They have to find money to pay off debt or bury their loved ones during stressful times. Planning after a family member has passed can be emotionally challenging for the rest of the family members. You want to give your family the best options possible, where they're not completely stressed if something may happen to you. Now I know this is a difficult topic to discuss. It's hard to bring it up to your family. But I think every family should be responsible enough to have family planning sessions and be connected to each family member, especially as you get older. Please take this part of your financial planning seriously.

Giving

There is something about giving that shifts a situation. When you're willing to let go of something from your hand that you need and even feel like you must hold on to it tightly, favor comes. It shifts your energy and allows money to flow to you freely because you made a choice to give. So, many times people say, "I don't have money to give," "I don't have enough," or "I can't afford to give," but the truth is you can't afford not to give. I think it's crucial for you to shift your perspective on what you have and don't have. God has given us so much. So, God asking for 10% for tithes and offering is nothing compared to what He's given us because He allows us to have 90%. The reality is that 100% of it belongs to Him anyway. He asks for 10% as a heart check. Are you willing to let go of a little to get a lot? This concept is not for everyone, and some may disagree, yet, giving has always existed. Be sure to give with an open heart. If you feel resentful or upset about giving, don't do it with a hard heart. Just keep it! God does not want you to give anything your heart is not fully into.

When you give sometimes, it doesn't always have to be monetary. Sometimes you can provide your time and or resources. Sometimes you can give your focus to helping someone else in their situation. You determine what that looks like for you and consult with God about what is on your heart. Sometimes it could be something as simple as paying for someone's groceries in the store or their prescription at the pharmacy. You apply a little bit of positive money energy to give to somebody else, ultimately increasing what's coming to you in the future. If you give, you will receive. If you think about somebody else for a second, something good will begin to come to you.

"God is the one who gives seed to the farmer and bread for food. He will give you all the seed you need to make it grow so there will be a great harvest from your goodness."
(2 Corinthians 9:10 NCV)

When you give, you let money know to grow, and when you give, you let God know He can trust you with more. I've often learned this perspective when I felt like I didn't have to give, yet I gave anyway. I have also paid for things for people I didn't even know, and every time that blessing has come back to me pressed down, shaken up, and running over. So my encouragement would be for you to look for opportunities to give instead of receiving or always telling yourself you don't have the money to give. How about from this point on, you start shifting your perspective? Wake up and start asking how I can give today. The universe will always respond to your questions when you ask whether you are providing your time, your giving money, your giving resources, or support. You just have to have a giving mindset when talking about shifting and healing your money mindset. You want to have a providing perspective to completely change where you are today. So, start this practice today, go and give.

"When you learn, teach, when you get give."
Dr. Maya Angelou.

Chapter 8

Principles of Dealing with Debt

"Do not owe people anything, except always owe love to each other, because the person who loves others has obeyed all the law."

(Romans 13:8, NCV)

Reducing Debt

How do you reduce debt? You reduce debt by slowly paying off debt and not accumulating new debt. It's not a unique formula for reducing your debt. First, you must consider where you are in your debt-paying process and always know your numbers. Then, review the debt you have and just start little by little. The best advice I could give is to simply begin. As you focus on paying your debt one at a time, start with the smallest, and you will gradually begin to see progress. For example, if you have something that's $100, go ahead and pay it off. Once the next month comes around, apply that $100 to whatever your next lowest bill is, and so on. The goal is to gradually reduce the total amount you owe and use the money you free up each month toward the next debt. There are also options to get 0% balance transfers to move debt to help pay it off quicker. Here's also the kicker, just don't go and get into more debt because this changes everything.

Often, I see people start and begin the process and have some good momentum paying off their debt, and then, for whatever situation or circumstance, they'll go and get into more debt. Living above your means and getting into more debt will set you back. Now I understand if it is due to a car issue or housing. However, try your best to stay on track. I have seen people who didn't have a car note buy a brand new car and put themselves in $30,000 or $40,000 in debt. This new debt also adjusts the monthly income by adding a sizable car note to monthly bills. At this point, you are working against your overall debt plan. In some situations, you have to purchase a newer car, right? We all need transportation. Always weigh your options. Was there an opportunity to buy a car outright? Or was there an opportunity to get a lower-cost car? You have to ask yourself these additional questions when trying to live and pay off debt simultaneously.

In my experience, most people have some kind of debt. Let's not feel bad about debt. I have worked with people who have negative feelings and emotions about debt. I have been coaching people for years, and no one is entirely out of debt in this day and time unless you are super-rich. There is a difference between actual debt and an investment in something that can make or save you money. You want to give yourself some grace around having debt. Also, know that you need to set up a plan to become debt-free because that gives you an actual plan for freedom. It releases you from the bondage of having to work jobs you don't want. You can pay for your living expense and maintain a particular lifestyle, but you don't have to worry about debt. As believers, God wants us to be debt-free. It's time we start invoking our kingdom rights. If you have substantial amounts of debt you're tied to, you must make different income decisions. There are situations where I know people that make significant incomes, six figures even, like lawyers, etc., but they have to maintain a particularly lavish lifestyle. Most of the time, they have large amounts of student loan debt because of their lifestyle and the debt they have accumulated. Some people are forced to choose to work jobs they hate to ensure they have the income to support their debt and lifestyle. So your goal should always be to reduce your debt and just your lifestyle to ensure you live within your means.

Life After Bankruptcy

I felt the need to talk about bankruptcy as a healing topic because I have worked with several people who filed for bankruptcy in the past. I notice people tend to feel bad about getting to this point in their finances. It's time to get past the shame and guilt you may feel if you've ever had to file for bankruptcy. I've worked with many people who had negative energy around money because they've had to decide to survive. I can say that nine out of ten people I've worked with that filed for bankruptcy didn't need to file. They had other options they were unaware of and other things that could have been done, but they waited too late.

There's always a decision and a choice to be made when you're considering what's next for you, and all options should be reviewed. I'm not saying that bankruptcy is not the right decision in some cases. It depends on the situation. What I can say is that I think you should exhaust all your other options before getting overwhelmed and making that kind of permanent decision. Working with a certified financial coach is always an option to help in these situations. In addition to that, there is also life after bankruptcy. Now, bankruptcy presents some long-term challenges with higher interest rates, possibly even denials in certain situations. However, some people continue to move forward and rebuild, even after bankruptcy. So if you've ever had to file for bankruptcy or consider it, let go of the shame or guilt behind it because other people have gone through the same thing.

Heal that trauma towards money so you can continue living. Also, if you haven't filed yet, just make sure you look into all your options before going down this road. Seek new knowledge when you're trying to rebuild. Ensure this clean slate gives you a fresh perspective. Understand that you will look at money and how you rebuild a little differently after going through bankruptcy. Also, look back over habits and behaviors that may have contributed to your situation so you don't repeat them again. Bankruptcy does not define you; you can and will get through this season of your life.

Debt-free Plan

Creating a debt-free plan is important. This plan helps you determine when you want to pay off specific bills. It should include the balance of the bills and the monthly payment amount. The easiest way is to first start with the lowest bill, considering the interest rate. So I have a mortgage currently. As I teach about finances and consult customers regularly about money, I'm still paying a mortgage and other debt. I plan to pay off my mortgage well before the 30-year mark, but in reality, I still have a mortgage, and I'm paying it every month. I still need to be connected to when that mortgage will be completely paid off. This will help save interest over time.

I want to know that because it helps me plan for my future and my retirement and prepare for a decision like whether I decide to sell my house or choose to rent it out later in life. You know, there are many different options when you own a home. You want to create a debt-free plan and what the debt-free plan looks like based on your goals. Your plan should include an outline of all the debt you want to pay off, how much you owe, and what date you want to pay that item off.

A debt-free plan gives you a vision and something to work towards. You can't aim for anything that you don't know the ultimate goal. If you don't know where you're going with something, it's hard for you to determine how to get to that place. You want to make sure that you're considering the ultimate goal, which can be for many things in your life, right? You must have a plan. You must have a target to aim towards. You have to know which direction you go to be able to obtain it. Paying off your debt is no different. We just get so consumed and overwhelmed when we see numbers. Sometimes, we get discouraged when we see how much debt we're looking at. Remember that this plan is worked on one piece at a time. With this plan, pay one debt at a time and don't get overwhelmed by the amount.

A quick example would be owing capital one $100. When can I pay that off? Or owing Wells Fargo $500. When can I pay that off? You just make it as plain as black and white until you're debt-free. If God asked you how much money you needed to be completely debt-free today, could you tell him?

Ensure you know your interest rates for all your debt and fully understand your payment information. This is key when you're talking about paying off debt. I see many clients who don't know the interest rate they're paying on a particular debt. They also don't understand how much of their payment is going toward interest and how much is going to the actual principal balance to pay off the debt. Knowing this is important because it can help you decide how to pay off debt.

The biggest thing is to pay off the lowest first, but you have to start making moves or having ideas when you know your payment amounts are primarily going somewhere with interest. I've seen situations where they focus on the payment amount. Let me make sure I can make this payment amount, but I need to save $400 a month. You have to consider whether that $400 needed to go to savings if you're paying an astronomical amount towards interest on a particular debt payment. Know your interest rates, numbers, and payment information. It's not that you have to know all the details. The biggest thing is to just be connected to the interest rates, so you can understand how and when to manage something different when it concerns your debt.

Chapter 9

Principles of Self-Reflection

"Look into your own hearts before you eat the bread and drink the cup because all who eat the bread and drink the cup without recognizing the body eat and drink judgment against themselves."
(1 Corinthians 11:28-29, NCV)

After reading this book, I want you to take the time to truly self-reflect. No one's perfect. And not even I am extremely, extremely good when it comes to money. I make mistakes every single day. I'm constantly learning and constantly evolving. The only difference is that I'm not willing to give up. One, I know God has more for me. Two, there's so much knowledge and resources in this world that I cannot sit and be stuck in an area of finances. You have to tell yourself that I've already been given the tools to succeed. It's no accident that you are reading this book. It's no accident you came along, read everything, and the details are part of the story. It was all intentional. And now, once you know the information, you can't go back to how you were. Knowledge is power, and our people perish for a simple lack of knowledge. But when your eyes are open, and you see the reality of some things, you cannot just sit back and act like you didn't see it.

You can't forget what you have seen. Once you have learned something, you can't unlearn what you have learned. Now you know the truth. You've also self-reflected on yourself, your mindset, and your feelings. You should have realized your part in where you are financially. To truly heal, ownership must happen. You also self-reflected on every aspect of knowledge when it comes to your budget when it comes to your credit. You also have set and dealt with your relationship with money. So now you're at the point where you get to choose. You get to choose your next step. You can continue down this path you've been on all this time and have the same outcome over and over again. Or you can do something different because you've learned something different. That time is now for change. And the reality is that this change is not just for you but for your entire family. God has more for you!

This change will impact everyone that's connected to you. And so, even though you are the one that read the book, even though you're the one that got the revelation and healing. The very things that you've learned can not only change the trajectory of your life, but they can change the trajectory of everyone's lives around you. So I didn't write this book just for me, although I learned a lot in my research and my revelation and writing this book, and I had my epiphanies of where I still was stuck in some areas. But I wrote this book to leave a legacy, to leave something to people who need a change and something different in their life but don't know where to go or what to do to change their financial situation.

So this book is for all those who grew up like me, from the hood but always had a dream. For all the people who grew up with a little, you still strived for better and learned along the way. For those who won't stop until you turn what you have into a lot. To all those that keep pressing forward no matter what, you just won't stop until you see the promises of God.

While I'm writing this book, we are currently going through a pandemic that has lasted for over two years. It's put a lot of stress on individuals regarding finances. We've seen a rise in everything. Gas is high, food is high, stocks are dropping, and housing cost is exceptionally high. Even simple things when you walk through the store cost way more than they used to. The inflation rate in the United States has risen over the past 12 months to an increase of 8.5%. It's the highest we've seen in the United States and over 40 years, and we are headed for a recession. Everything is out of alignment.

Despite the circumstances, millions of people walked away from their jobs this year, searching for more. Searching for peace and a better quality of life. It comes a time when you have to reflect on where you are, so you can plan where you need to go. I don't see much of this changing anytime soon, and I see the country's financial situation getting worse before it gets better. We have to adjust now to either increase income or find ways to decrease debt for us to be able to survive. We must also prepare for the future and help the next generation. The biggest thing I want people of faith to know is that God will always provide for you, but He did give you understanding and revelation to seek knowledge, and our people perish for lack of knowledge. Part of this is for us to understand where we are, take that knowledge, and be able to do something about changing our future quickly.

Discipline

If you want to change your situation for the long term, it requires discipline. There is no way around it. Even when you make a lot of money, the money won't last long if you don't operate with some form of discipline.

Anything in life that you desire to improve takes focus and determination. For example, suppose you want to lose weight and get healthier. In that case, you must become more disciplined around your workout routine, food, and overall health.

Remember, this is an ongoing process that doesn't happen overnight. The key is staying focused, sticking to your budget, and setting and tracking your goals. The truth is your discipline is more than half the battle. Even if you mess up, you can make a choice right where you are to start focusing on your situation at hand. No judgment, don't beat yourself up. Just focus on where you are going, not where you are or where you have been. Once you become more disciplined with your finances, you will start thinking differently and your thoughts will gradually shift so will your habits and behaviors.

Chapter 10

Principles of Having Support

"By helping each other with your troubles,
you truly obey the law of Christ."
(Galatians 6:2, NCV)

You Are Not Alone

If you're struggling with money or have ever struggled with money, you are not alone.

There are many people that I work with and many people that I know that struggle when it comes to money. Unfortunately, intentional money conversations are not held in our households. People grow up in a home not understanding how their parents are spending their money or even knowing about household bills are paid etc. They do, however, end up understanding when mom or dad gets the next paycheck because those days are reward days. There are entrepreneurs I know that have businesses that aren't even able to pay themselves in their business because of the profits not allowing payroll, even though the business may make a significant income. So again, if this is you as an entrepreneur, you are not alone.

They need every penny they have just to continue making the business survive. So they're operating and working in their dream, but the reality may feel like they have created another form of slavery. So, again you're not alone. People every day get up and work hard, yet they still struggle. Sometimes the challenging part is that we don't even ask for help. We don't talk about what we're going through because we feel like we are the only ones going through a difficult situation, and we feel embarrassed. We feel like nobody understands our circumstances, and we feel ashamed.

We think people will judge us if we start talking about how we're struggling and can't afford something. The sad part is that those who do have money don't want to say anything because they don't want people to start asking them for money. The reality is that we need to seek help and support to move forward. We need to seek knowledge and resources. We must start looking for better opportunities and ways to improve our situation. But we can't do it all alone. It is hard to change a situation on our own when we're not talking about what's happening. So, I hope to start having more conversations about money in our culture and communities. I hope it becomes a normal conversation in every household and we teach our children. I hope our children start learning more about finances in schools and college. I hope they know the impact of student loans, credit cards, and life insurance. Knowledge will help so that we don't regret decisions made while we are young. We needed to educate people on money and these other different resources.

So after this, just know you're not alone. Know that other people like you may be in the same or a different situation. Some have recovered and gone on to improve their lives, and some haven't. I haven't always made the best decisions and choices in life and with money, if I'm honest. But what I do know is that my God supplies all my needs, and I appreciate all His resources. So when I look back over my life, even in situations where I did struggle, one thing I know is I always survived. Another thing I learned is I was never alone. So hopefully, this will offer you some relief, peace, and hope, knowing that no matter your situation, you can move past it, get out of it, and move forward.

Chapter 11

Next Steps- Money Plans

"People may make plans in their minds, yet only the Lord can make them come true."
(Proverbs 16:1, NCV)

Create Your Plans

Now it's time for you to look at your current situation. The question is simple: Are you where you want or need to be financially? If not, what do you plan to do about it? It's time for you to create change in your life. It's time to start your plan. What's your money improvement plan? Look at the list below and set up a plan for each item needed in your life for the next 30 days, 90 days, 3-6 months, 6-12 months, 1-5 years, etc.

Emergency Savings Plan: minimum $1,000

Regular Savings Plan: minimum 6 months of expenses

Investing/ stocks, index funds, mutual, funds Plan

Insurance Plan

Paying off debt Plan

Retirement Plan

Improving credit Plan

Homeowner's Plan

Increasing income Plan

Starting business Plan

New Job Plan

New resume Plan

Other options for growth:

- Financial Education
- Financial Coaching
- Accountability Group

Are you ready to commit to something new?

I know it's hard to change your mind about things you have done for as long as you can remember, but I have seen people do it repeatedly. I have transformed my own life from that little girl in the hood to now having a successful career, teaching about money, and writing this book. Where I come from, people don't even read books, let alone write them, but it's time to change the game. It's time to live your best life, change the path for your family, and take control of your finances.

You deserve a life of overflow and abundance. You deserve the best, and when you work hard at your goals, there is nothing that can stop you from changing your situation. This is your season to prosper, but there are some things you may need to change or do differently. I pray that something you read in this book inspires you to act and change your thoughts, habits, and behaviors to eventually change your life.

Chapter 12

Money Prayer

"What you say can mean life or death"
(Proverbs 18:21, NCV)

"Be careful what you think, because
your thoughts run your life."
(Proverbs 4:23, NCV)

My prayer for the person reading this is that you know you are worth it. You are worth the work you put into yourself, your growth, and your development. You are worth the wealth coming your way, and you embrace that abundance is your birthright. I pray that you expand your mind and open up your heart to receive what you have learned in this book, even the difficult things you embraced. I pray that even the things you may not have understood at the moment, you receive a revelation at the right moment. I know that you know some of these things you've never even heard about or understood because some just don't talk about finances. I pray that your life has changed and that you somehow see things differently because of the information you have received. I hope the trajectory of your life will change and you understand that God is for you and wants you to prosper. I pray that once you begin to implement things from this book, you will be able to help break generational curses around money. I pray that you no longer live in a lack mindset in any area of your life and that you no longer live in a place where you feel like the world is against you. I hope you embrace every aspect of who you are and go after the things you want. I want you to continue to thrive and live abundantly. Embrace the idea that money loves you, is attracted to you, and is your friend. Money will give you the ability to be able to be utilized and help change the world.

I pray that your energy with money is healed, that your lack of mindset is healed. I hope you think of new ideas, new inventions, and new ways to make money and better your situation like never before. I pray that the next few months in this next realm of your life will be different. I pray that no matter your struggle with money or your pain with money, no matter your situation, you now have a clean slate. I pray for your elevation and favor on your job and in your business. I pray that you see God's best from this point on. Know that money is a resource and avoid this idealism that money is evil. The truth is, the LOVE of money is evil. I pray that you don't love anything more than God. Guard your heart. God doesn't want anything before Him, no idols. The truth is that God wants us to be rich. He wants us to be wealthy. He already said He's moving the wealth from the wicked to the righteous, but you have to be prepared to receive what He's doing in this next season. I pray that you prepare for this shift that's about to happen. Start with healing your mindset. Know you are valuable. You can no longer operate in a charity mindset in this season. God needs you to think with your CEO mindset. I pray that you practice the budget you put in place and the things you need to grow and nurture in this lifetime. I rebuke the generational curse of a lack of mindset about money in my culture and community. It starts with this one prayer. Amen!

Money Mindset Exercise

Create your own money affirmations, mantras, or lofty questions

"God who gives life to the dead and calls into being things that were not."

(Romans 4:17, NIV)

There is power in your words. You should speak life into your life daily, but you must command your money. When you are going through the process of shifting your money mindset, you must be intentional about affirming your situation. Try your best not to speak negative words over your money and begin speaking only positive words. No matter how you feel, this should be a daily practice in your life.

Create at least three money affirmations, money mantras, or lofty questions to speak over your life. I have provided a few examples below:

1. I will focus on my finances.
2. Growth in this area will happen when I'm focused.
3. I'm a good steward over what I have, and money flows to me freely today.
4. I am a magnet for increase, wealth, and prosperity.
5. Abundance is coming to me now because it's my birthright
6. My job is a resource; God is my source.
7. Wealth is already mine. I can see it. I can touch it. I can feel it.
8. Why am I so wealthy?
9. I'm already rich.
10. I'm already living my best life.

11. Why is money attracted to me?

12. Why is money so attached to me?

13. Why is money chasing me down today?

14. Money flows freely money flows freely. Money flows freely to me.

15. Why do I have the most amazing relationship with money?

Pick 3-4 or create your own to speak daily.

So, at this moment, as you wrap up this book, I hope that you embrace the change and that your life will never be the same. And that because of what you've done and your decisions, you and your family's life will never be the same.

About the Author

Jeanette Barnette grew up in the inner city of Baltimore, Maryland. After growing up in a city overwhelmed with poverty, she was determined to create a better life for herself. Jeanette has 10+ years of experience in the banking and finance industry, working in several positions for large banks like Regions Bank and Bank of America. In addition, she has a BS degree in Human Resources. She is certified as a financial coach by Dave Ramsey, certified as a life coach through Mindvalley, and certified in biblical studies by Dr. Darius Daniels.

Jeanette moved to Atlanta, GA, purchased her first house at the age of 23, and got married with dreams of living happily ever after; however, her marriage didn't last, and she ended up divorced and struggling. Due to the circumstance, Jeanette also ended up with 90% of the debt accumulated in her marriage. She wiped out her savings, ruined her credit, and faced foreclosure. Jeanette has also had her share of health challenges, from high stroke level blood pressure to diabetes and even a long process of cancer screenings and testing. During this time, Jeanette also committed her life to God and trusted His will and way for her life.

Jeanette did several things to get her life back on track, like going to college, tripling her income, rebuilding her credit, and maintaining a strict budget to achieve financial milestones. She also has committed to a healthier lifestyle of working out consistently and meal prepping, and self-care.

She has successfully rebuilt her life one piece at a time. She has increased her credit score to excellent, paid off thousands of dollars in debt, and has been a homeowner for 15 years. She has also successfully reduced her blood pressure medications and reversed her diabetes. She is now also a financial coach and wants to help other people obtain their milestones on health & wealth, shift their mindsets, and gain a new level of freedom.

References

- "Aliche, Tiffany. "5" Get Good with Money: Ten Simple Steps to Becoming Financially Whole, Harmony Books, New York, NY, 2021,
- Kimbro, Dennis, et al. "1." Think and Grow Rich: A Black Choice, Fawcett Columbine, New York, New York, 1997

Made in the USA
Monee, IL
04 November 2026

67376118R00069